JR. GRAPHIC ANCIENT CIVILIZATIONS

EVERYDAY LIFE IN
ANCIENT
ROME

KIRSTEN HOLM

PowerKiDS
press™

New York

Published in 2012 by The Rosen Publishing Group, Inc.

29 East 21st Street, New York, NY 10010

First Edition

Editor: Joanne Randolph

Book Design: Planman Technologies

Illustrations: Planman Technologies

Library of Congress Cataloging-in-Publication Data

Holm, Kirsten C. (Kirsten Campbell)

Everyday life in Ancient Rome / by Kirsten Holm. — 1st ed.

   p. cm. — (Jr. graphic ancient civilizations)

Includes index.

ISBN 978-1-4488-6215-3 (library binding) — ISBN 978-1-4488-6389-1 (pbk.) — ISBN 978-1-4488-6390-7 (6-pack)

1. Rome—Civilization—Juvenile literature. 2. Rome—Civilization—Comic books, strips, etc. 3. Graphic novels. I. Title.

DG77.H59 2012

937—dc23

2011020650

Manufactured in the United States of America

CPSIA Compliance Information: Batch #PLW2102PK: For Further Information contact Rosen Publishing, New York, New York at 1-800-237-9932.

Contents

Main Characters

Emperor Lucius Septimus Severus. AD 145–AD 211. Severus was born in Leptis Magna, Africa, a prominent Roman city about 80 miles (130 km) east of Tripoli in the current-day country of Libya. He was appointed senator in AD 175 and served as both governor and consul. In AD 193, Severus became emperor. In Rome, he was known as a skilled administrator and increased both the size of the Roman police forces and the city's fire brigades. A military man throughout his life, Severus led successful military campaigns while serving as emperor. He is known as the founder of the Severan dynasty.

Overview

- The Roman Empire began with Augustus in 27 BC and lasted for another 500 years.

- By AD 200, the Roman Empire covered most of the Middle East, stretched over northern Africa and half of Europe, including Britain. The empire was about the size of the United States.

- Approximately 1 million people lived in the city of Rome.

- Roman **citizens** were divided into classes, or ranks, depending upon their wealth and land holdings. Patricians formed the top rank. They were wealthy and owned land. Many served in the Senate. **Equestrians** were wealthy citizens, many of whom had served in the army and held administrative posts in the empire. The bottom rank was comprised of ordinary, working-class citizens called **plebeians**. Slaves were not citizens.

- Slavery was a common practice throughout the Roman Empire, and wealthy Romans would own a large number of household slaves, including cooks, gardeners, household help, accountants, and tutors for their children.

EVERYDAY LIFE IN
ANCIENT ROME

ROME, AD 202

ALL MALE ROMAN CITIZENS WERE REQUIRED TO SERVE IN THE MILITARY. THE ARMY WAS A **DISCIPLINED**, FIERCE FIGHTING FORCE.

WEALTHY ROMANS LIVED IN ORNATE VILLAS THAT HAD FRESCOED WALLS, MOSAIC FLOORS, AND BEAUTIFUL GARDENS.

I AM GLAD YOU ARE HOME SAFE AND IN ONE PIECE.

I WILL BE STAYING IN ROME NOW. THE EMPEROR HAS ASKED ME TO LEAD THE PRAETORIAN GUARDS.

ROMAN FATHERS HAD THEIR OWN STUDIES, CALLED *TABLINA*, WHERE THEY TOOK CARE OF HOUSEHOLD BUSINESS.

YOU HAVE KEPT CAREFUL ACCOUNTS WHILE I WAS GONE.

I HOPE YOU ARE PLEASED. NOW, THOUGH, YOUR CHILDREN ARE WAITING FOR YOU.

WE MISSED YOU, FATHER. I AM GLAD YOU ARE HOME.

I AM GLAD TO BE HOME, TOO.

SOME ROMAN WOMEN WORKED, BUT MANY STAYED AT HOME, TEACHING THEIR CHILDREN AND RUNNING THE HOUSEHOLD.

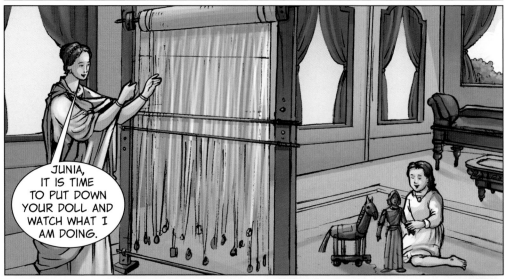

JUNIA, IT IS TIME TO PUT DOWN YOUR DOLL AND WATCH WHAT I AM DOING.

PAY CAREFUL ATTENTION. SOON YOU WILL NEED TO WEAVE BY YOURSELF.

NOW YOU TRY IT, JUNIA. A FEW YEARS FROM NOW, YOU WILL MARRY AND BE WEAVING CLOTH FOR YOUR OWN FAMILY.

ROMAN GIRLS WERE TAUGHT AT HOME, BOTH BY THEIR MOTHERS AND BY EDUCATED SLAVES.

YOUNG BOYS LEARNED TO READ, WRITE, AND DO SIMPLE ARITHMETIC AT HOME. FROM AGES 7 TO 16, BOYS FROM WEALTHY FAMILIES WENT TO SCHOOL.

IT IS TIME FOR YOU TO LEARN FROM A TUTOR, NOT JUST YOUR MOTHER AND ME.

I HAVE LOTS TO LEARN, BUT I HOPE WE HAVE TIME FOR GAMES, TOO.

IN ADDITION TO READING, WRITING, AND ARITHMETIC, BOYS LEARNED TO SERVE AS SOLDIERS.

I'VE GOT YOU NOW. I WIN THIS BATTLE!

THESE ARE THE WEAPONS THE ARMY USES. WHO CAN THROW THE JAVELIN THE FARTHEST?

CITIZENS OF ALL RANKS COULD PRESENT THEIR PERSONAL REQUESTS, CALLED **PETITIONS**, TO THE EMPEROR.

THE FORUM WAS A LARGE CENTRAL PLAZA THAT HOUSED MANY GOVERNMENT BUILDINGS. IT WAS A LIVELY PLACE WHERE CITIZENS MET TO DISCUSS EVENTS OF THE DAY.

WE MUST HURRY. WE ARE TO MEET THE EMPEROR AT THE FORUM. HE MEETS WITH THE SENATE THIS MORNING.

WE WILL GUARD THE EMPEROR AND THE SENATORS.

THESE ARE BUSY, CROWDED STREETS, AND I HEAR THIEVES ARE DOING VERY WELL THESE DAYS.

WE KNOW WHAT TO WATCH FOR AND WHAT TO DO.

WATCH EVERYONE. THE EMPEROR WILL ARRIVE SOON, AND THERE ARE PEOPLE FROM ALL OVER THE EMPIRE HERE TODAY.

IT IS TIME TO TURN OUR THOUGHTS FROM WAR TO MAKING LIFE BETTER FOR ROMAN CITIZENS HERE AT HOME.

IT HAS BEEN THREE HOURS ALREADY. HOW LONG CAN THIS LAST?

THE SENATE WILL BREAK FOR LUNCH SOON.

FINALLY, WE GET TO EAT SOME LUNCH. I BOUGHT SOME FISH AND OLIVES.

I HOPE YOU HAVE TIME TO EAT. THOSE TWO MEN ARE FIGHTING.

HE STOLE MY MONEY!

SETTLE DOWN. YOU ARE ONLY MAKING IT WORSE FOR YOURSELF.

NOT A BAD WAY TO END THE DAY. THE EMPEROR IS SAFELY BACK AT THE PALACE, AND WE CAUGHT A THIEF. NOW I HAVE TO HEAD FOR HOME.

ROMANS ATE THEIR MAIN MEAL IN THE LATE AFTERNOON. WEALTHY ROMANS USUALLY ENDED THEIR DAY GIVING OR ATTENDING **BANQUETS**. DINNERS INCLUDED AT LEAST THREE COURSES.

GENERAL, TELL US ABOUT YOUR CAMPAIGN IN AFRICA.

ONE OF OUR FIRST DUTIES WAS TO BUILD A FORT TO PROTECT OURSELVES AND TO SERVE AS A BASE FOR WARFARE.

"OUR WEAPONS AND GEAR WERE HEAVY.

"WHEN WE WEREN'T FIGHTING, WE BUILT ROADS AND AQUEDUCTS. ROMAN SOLDIERS ARE THE BEST BUILDERS IN THE WORLD."

ROMANS DID NOT SIT AT TABLES TO EAT, THEY RECLINED ON COUCHES. SLAVES PREPARED AND SERVED THE FOOD.

PLEASE JOIN US IN THIS SIMPLE DINNER.

I WOULD HARDLY CALL IT SIMPLE. IT LOOKS AS IF WE WILL HAVE A FEAST.

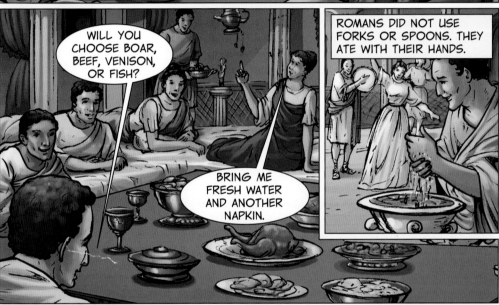

WILL YOU CHOOSE BOAR, BEEF, VENISON, OR FISH?

BRING ME FRESH WATER AND ANOTHER NAPKIN.

ROMANS DID NOT USE FORKS OR SPOONS. THEY ATE WITH THEIR HANDS.

THANKS FOR A LOVELY EVENING. WILL YOU BE JOINING THE EMPEROR AT THE COLOSSEUM TOMORROW? PERHAPS I WILL SEE YOU THERE.

OUR SLAVES WILL SEE YOU HOME.

ROMANS LOVED TO BE ENTERTAINED AT THE COLOSSEUM, MOCK NAVAL BATTLES WERE STAGED. **GLADIATORS** FOUGHT EACH OTHER AND WILD ANIMALS. SUCCESSFUL GLADIATORS WERE SOMETIMES ABLE TO WIN THEIR FREEDOM.

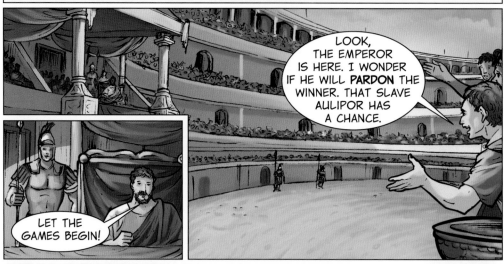

LOOK, THE EMPEROR IS HERE. I WONDER IF HE WILL **PARDON** THE WINNER. THAT SLAVE AULIPOR HAS A CHANCE.

LET THE GAMES BEGIN!

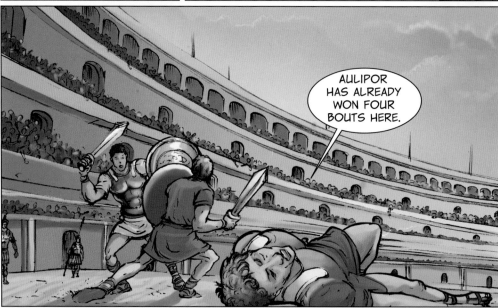

AULIPOR HAS ALREADY WON FOUR BOUTS HERE.

LONG LIVE THE EMPEROR!

AULIPOR IS NOW A FREEDMAN. I HEAR THE EMPEROR IS GOING TO THE **CHARIOT** RACES NEXT.

CHARIOT RACES WERE HIGH SPEED AND RISKY. THE TRACK WAS NARROW, AND THE TURNS WERE SMALL AND TIGHT.

WHICH CHARIOT TEAM DO YOU THINK WILL WIN TODAY?

THE EMPEROR SUPPORTS THE GREENS. I AM ROOTING FOR THEM, TOO.

GO, GREENS!

GO, GREENS!

GO, GREENS!

IT WAS A WELL-RUN RACE. NO HORSES FELL AND NO CHARIOTS WERE OVERTURNED.

I AM GLAD THIS IS OVER. THE EMPEROR IS GOING BACK TO THE PALACE, AND I NEED SOME TIME TO MYSELF.

MEN AND WOMEN WENT EVERY DAY TO THE BATHS TO BATHE, RELAX, EXERCISE, AND MEET WITH FRIENDS. THEY USED OLIVE OIL INSTEAD OF SOAP.

AFTER A LONG DAY IN THE SUN, THIS IS THE BEST.

BATHHOUSES WERE THE SCENES FOR CONCERTS AND POETRY READINGS.

BATHHOUSES HAD GYMNASIUMS AND BALL COURTS, TOO. ROMANS VALUED EXERCISE AND WENT TO GYMNASIUMS DAILY.

ROMANS LOVED BOTH GREEK TRAGEDIES AND ROMAN COMEDIES. THEY ALSO CAME TO THE THEATER TO WATCH **MIMES** AND **PANTOMIMES**.

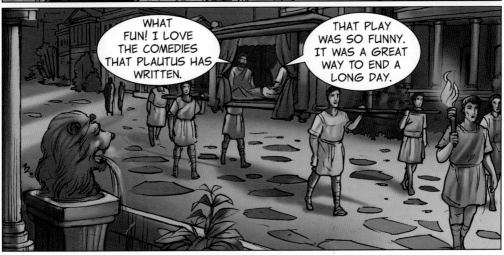

ON YOUR SIXTEENTH BIRTHDAY, YOU WILL **REGISTER** AS A CITIZEN. I HAVE DECIDED THAT UNTIL THEN, YOU WILL CONTINUE YOUR STUDIES HERE IN ROME.

FINALLY, I AM AN ADULT, READY TO SERVE MY COUNTRY.

I WANT TO SERVE IN THE ARMY, JUST AS MY FATHER DID.

YOU ARE JUST A CHILD NOW, BUT YOUR FATHER AND I WILL SOON BE SELECTING YOUR HUSBAND.

I HOPE YOU WILL LET ME HAVE A SAY IN THE CHOICE.

ROMAN WEDDINGS WERE SIMPLE, BUT THEY WERE FOLLOWED BY **LAVISH** FEASTS, WHICH CELEBRATED THE NEWLYWEDS.

ONE DAY SOON YOU WILL HAVE YOUR OWN HOME, YOUR OWN CHILDREN, AND YOUR OWN SLAVES. THIS IS ROMAN LIFE.

Did You Know?

- Wealthy Roman boys went to school beginning at age seven. The school day began early in the morning and lasted until noon. Girls did not go to school. They were educated at home.

- While wealthy Romans lived in lavish homes and villas, poor Romans lived in apartment buildings. These buildings were usually five to six stories tall and often had shops on the ground floor. The buildings had no running water or indoor plumbing.

- Rome had fire brigades to watch for and put out fires within the city.

- Roman women wore makeup. They used chalk to make their skin white and colored their lips and cheeks red. They also lined their eyes and eyebrows with black. They sometimes dyed their hair and had hairdos with coiled braids and lots of curls.

- Women had some rights, but they could not vote.

- Roman men, until the second century, were clean shaven. Then beards became fairly popular.

- Both men and women wore jewelry, including necklaces and rings.

- The Romans were religious. They believed in many gods. Many homes had small shrines to honor their household gods, which were to believed to keep the home safe.

Glossary

banquets (BAN-kwets) Large meals eaten in honor of holidays or special events. Wealthy Romans frequently hosted banquets.

chariot (CHAR-ee-ut) A two-wheeled battle car pulled by horses.

citizens (SIH-tih-zenz) People who were born in or who have the right to live in a country or other community. In Rome, citizenship meant having rights, including the right to vote, that were denied to others.

disciplined (DIH-sih-plind) Highly trained or developed by teaching and exercise.

equestrians (ih-KWES-tree-unz) A class of wealthy Roman citizens.

gladiator (GLA-dee-ay-tur) A person who fought to the death against other men or animals.

lavish (LA-vish) Excessive, or going beyond what is considered normal.

mimes (MYMZ) In Roman theater, the humorous retelling of a story, usually scenes from everyday life.

pantomimes (PAN-tuh-mymz) Telling a story without words, using body movements and facial expressions. In Roman theater, actors in pantomimes often used masks to show facial expressions.

pardon (PAR-dun) To excuse someone who did something wrong.

petitions (puh-TIH-shunz) Formal ways to ask for something to be done.

plebeians (pluh-BE-unz) A class of common citizens of Rome.

Praetorian Guards (pree-TAWR-ee-un GAHRDZ) Men who helped keep the city of Rome and the Roman emperor safe.

protection (pruh-TEK-shun) Something that keeps something else from being hurt.

reign (RAYN) To rule or to hold office as the head of the government.

register (REH-jih-ster) To sign an official record book.

Index

Web Sites

Due to the changing nature of Internet links, PowerKids Press has developed an online list of Web sites related to the subject of this book. This site is updated regularly. Please use this link to access the list:

www.powerkidslinks.com/civi/rome/